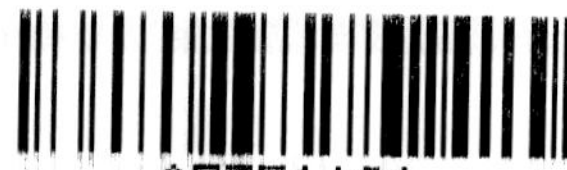

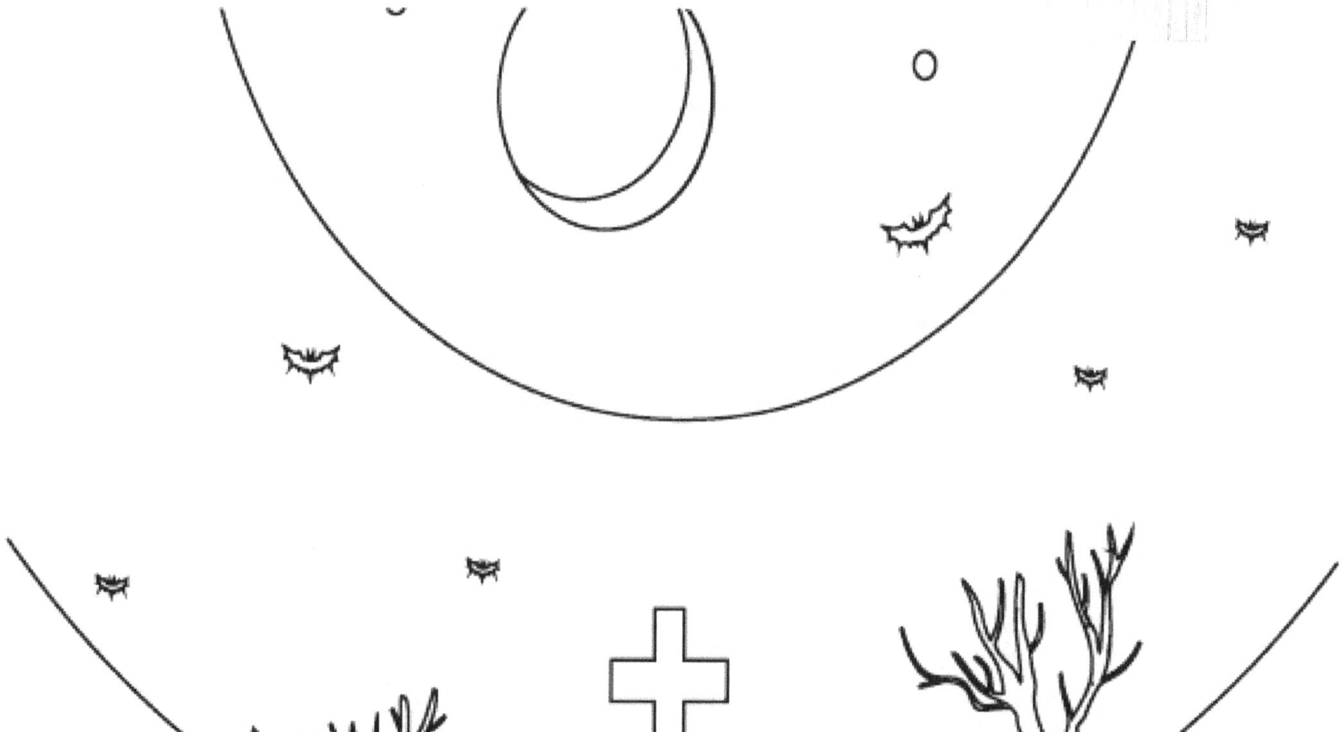

HALLOWEEN
COLORING BOOK FOR TEENS

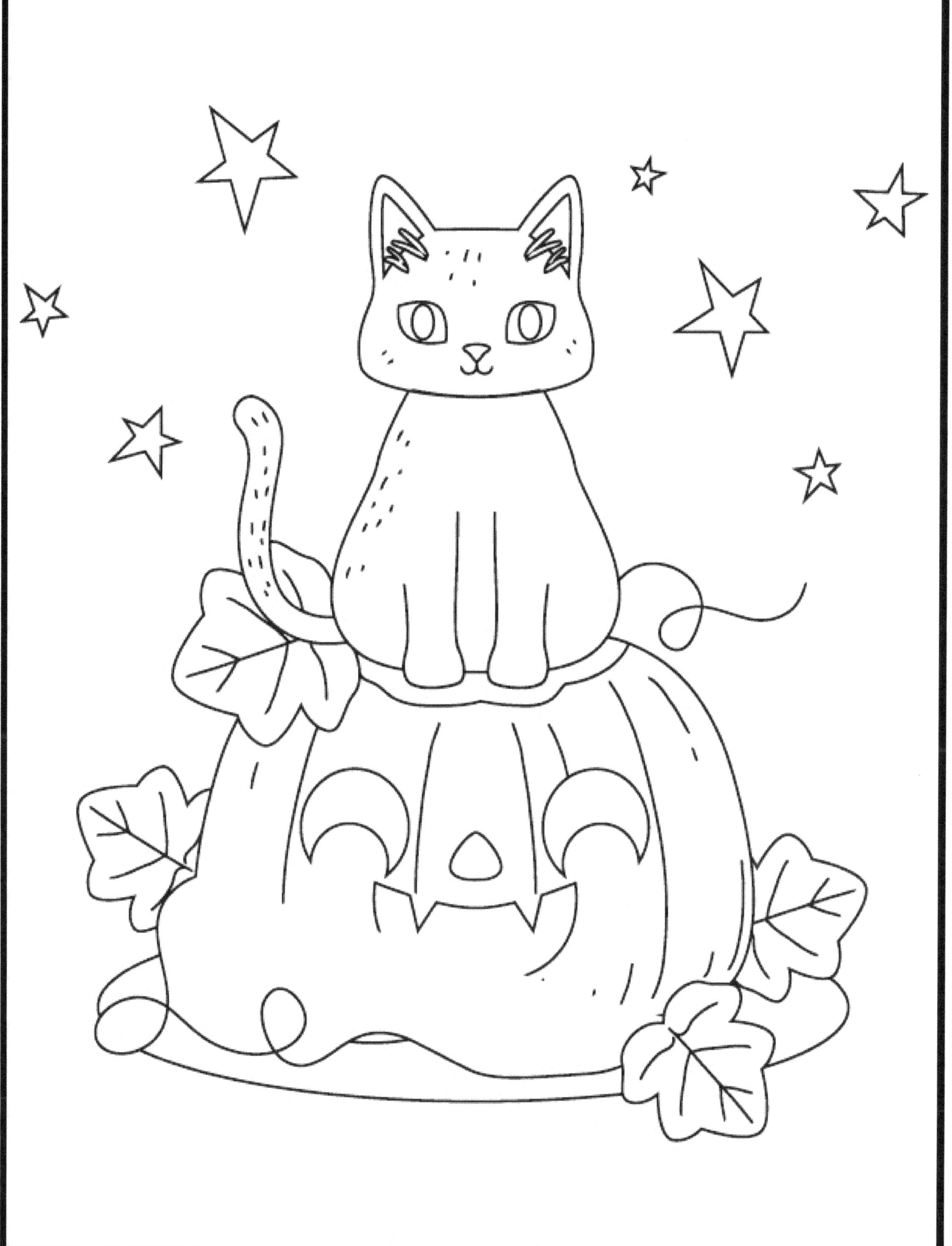

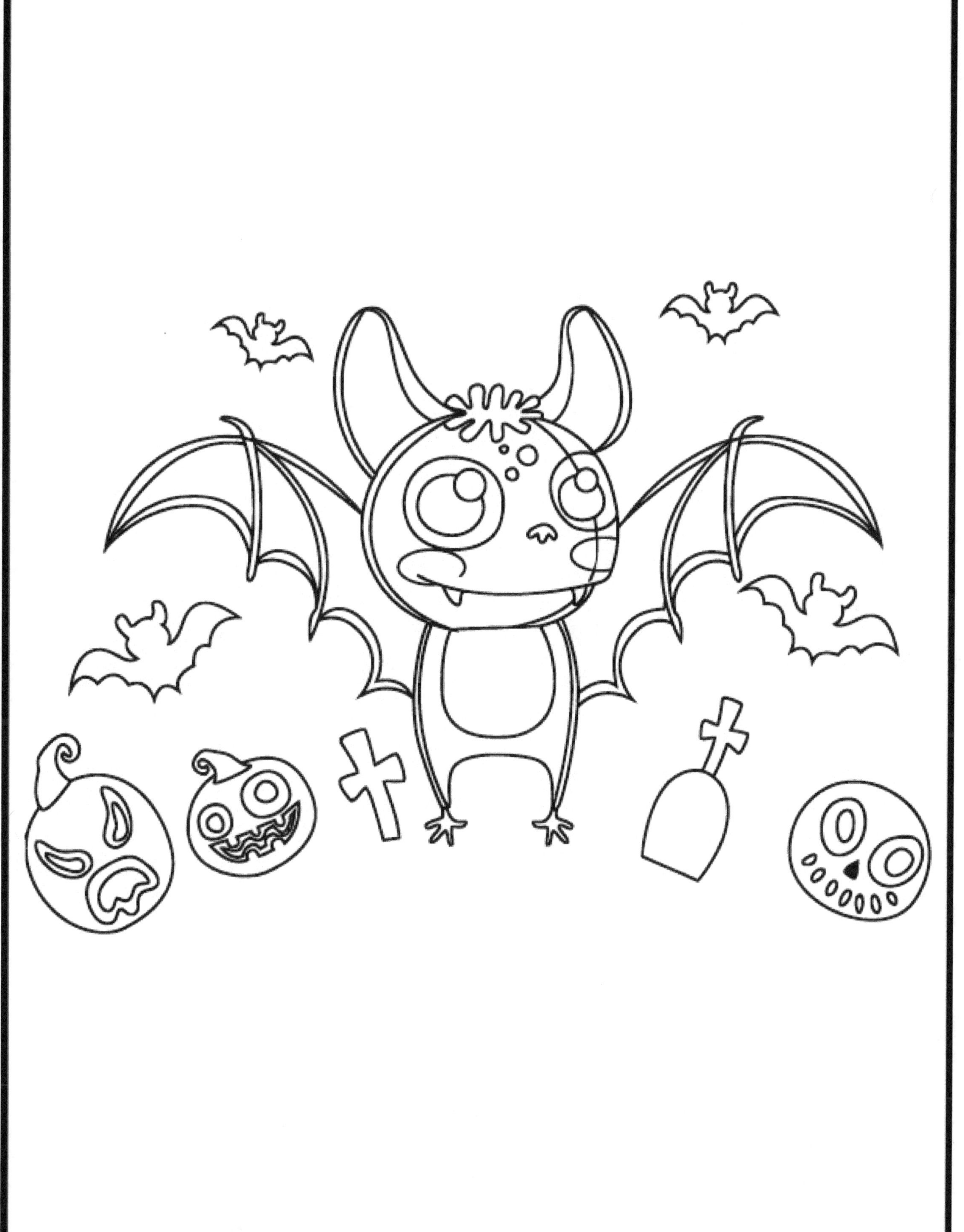

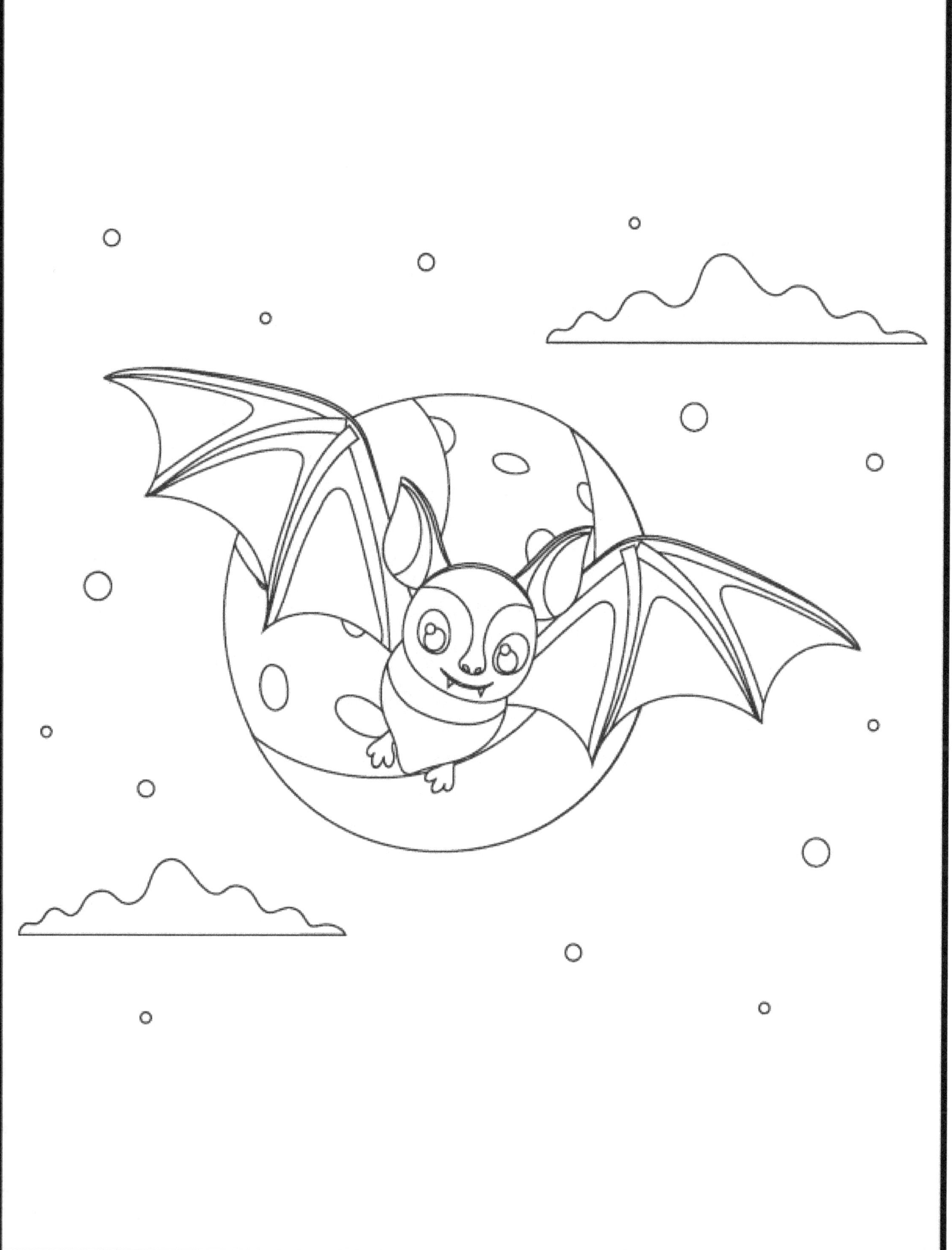

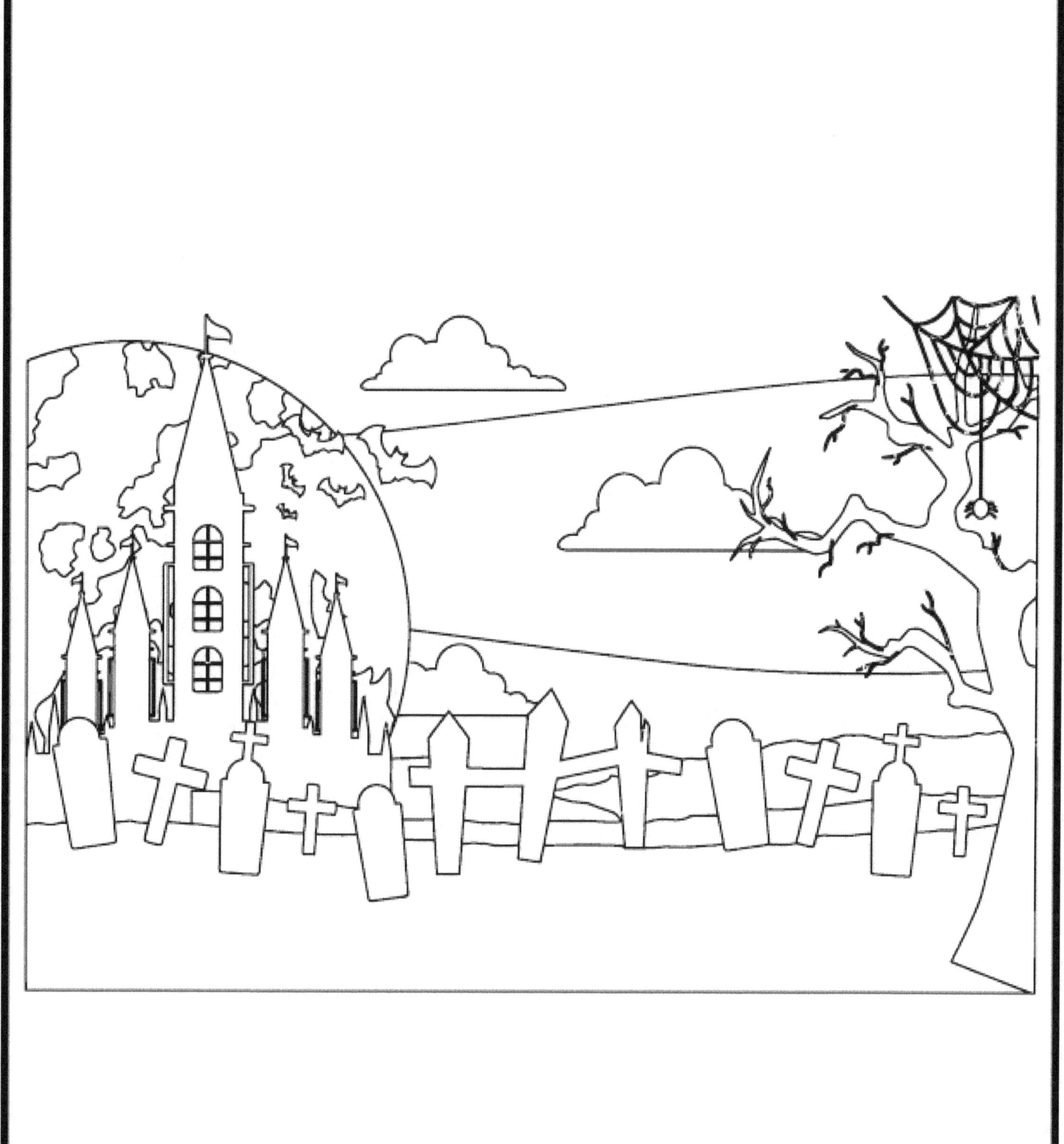

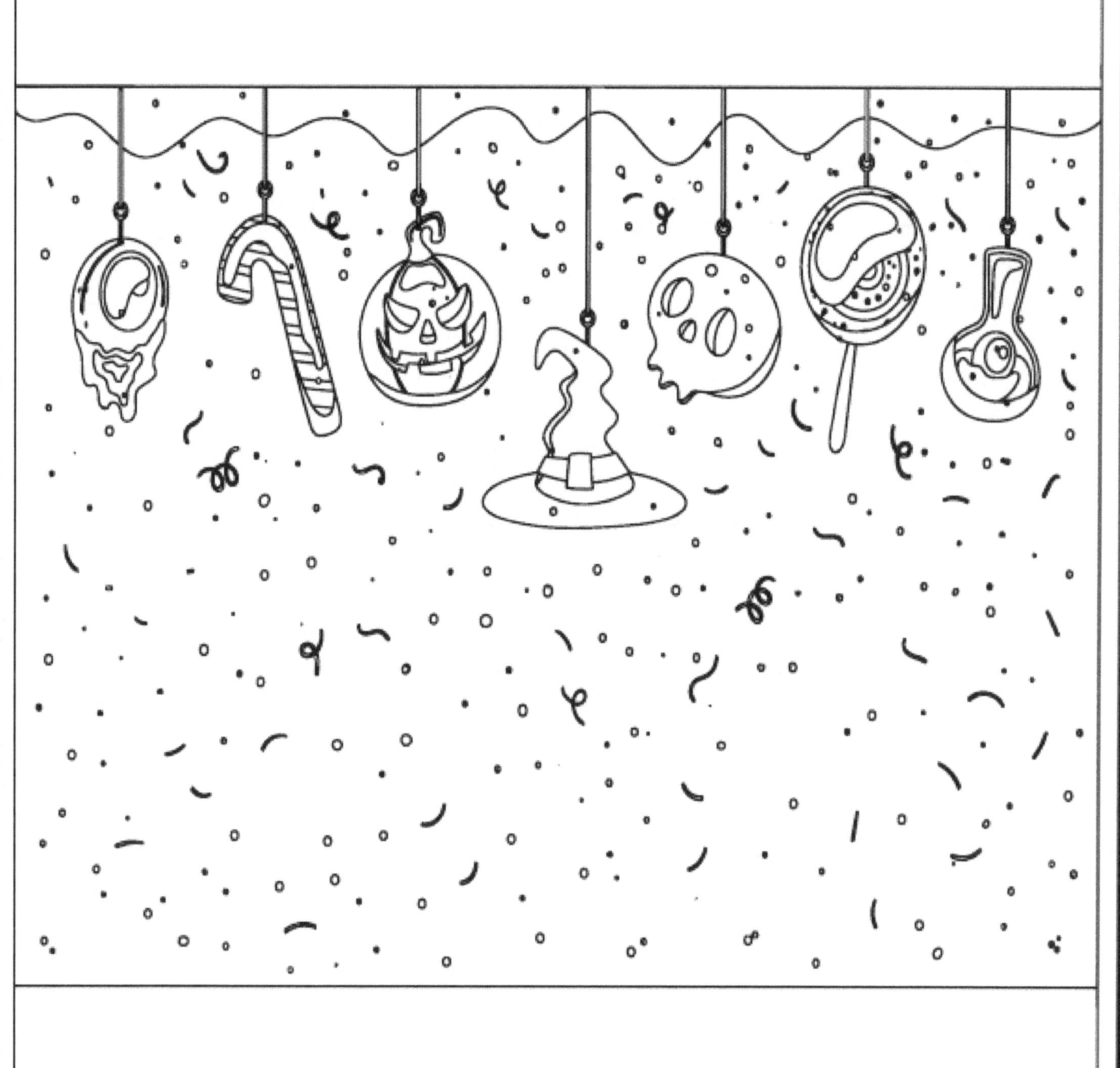

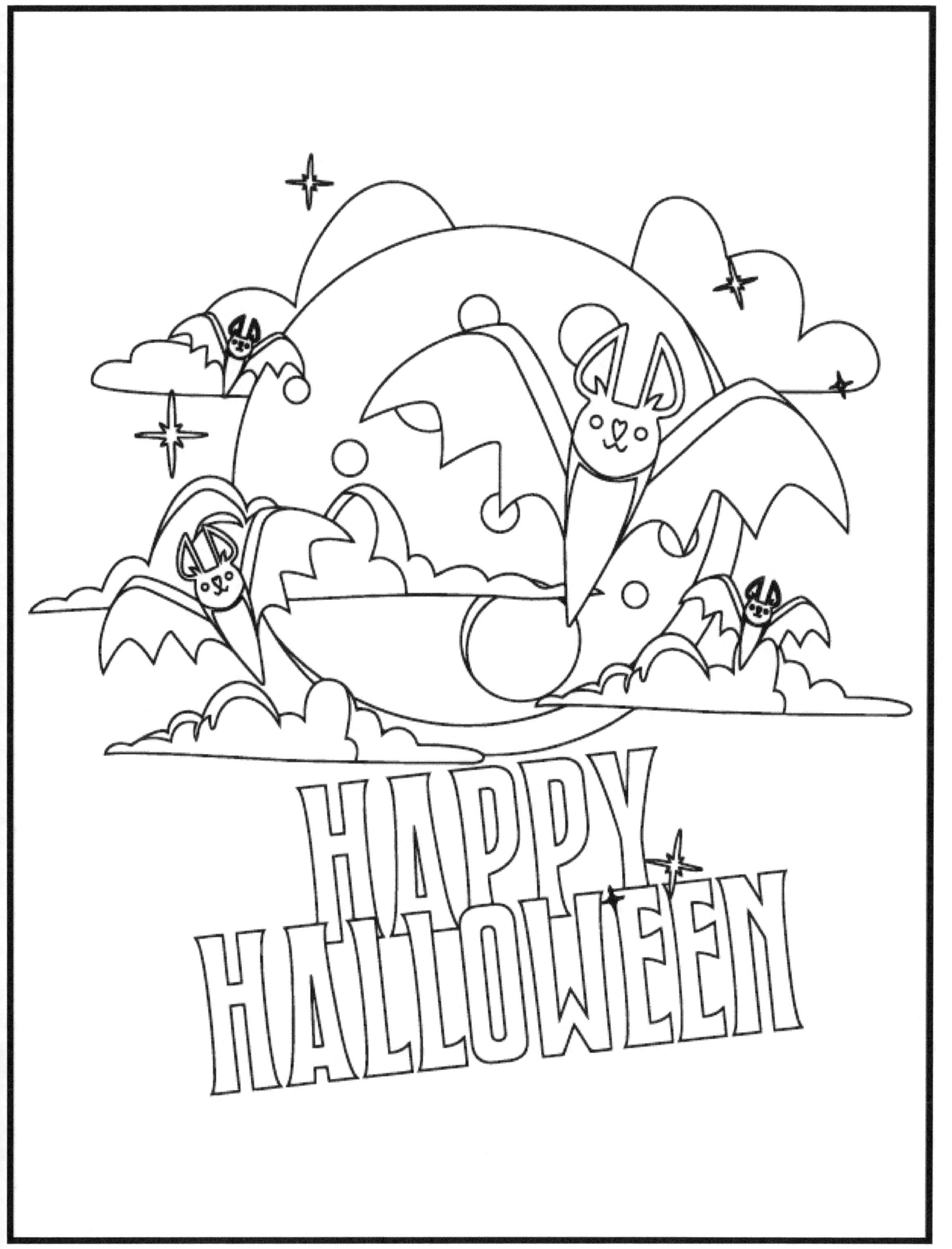

HAPPY
HALLOWEEN

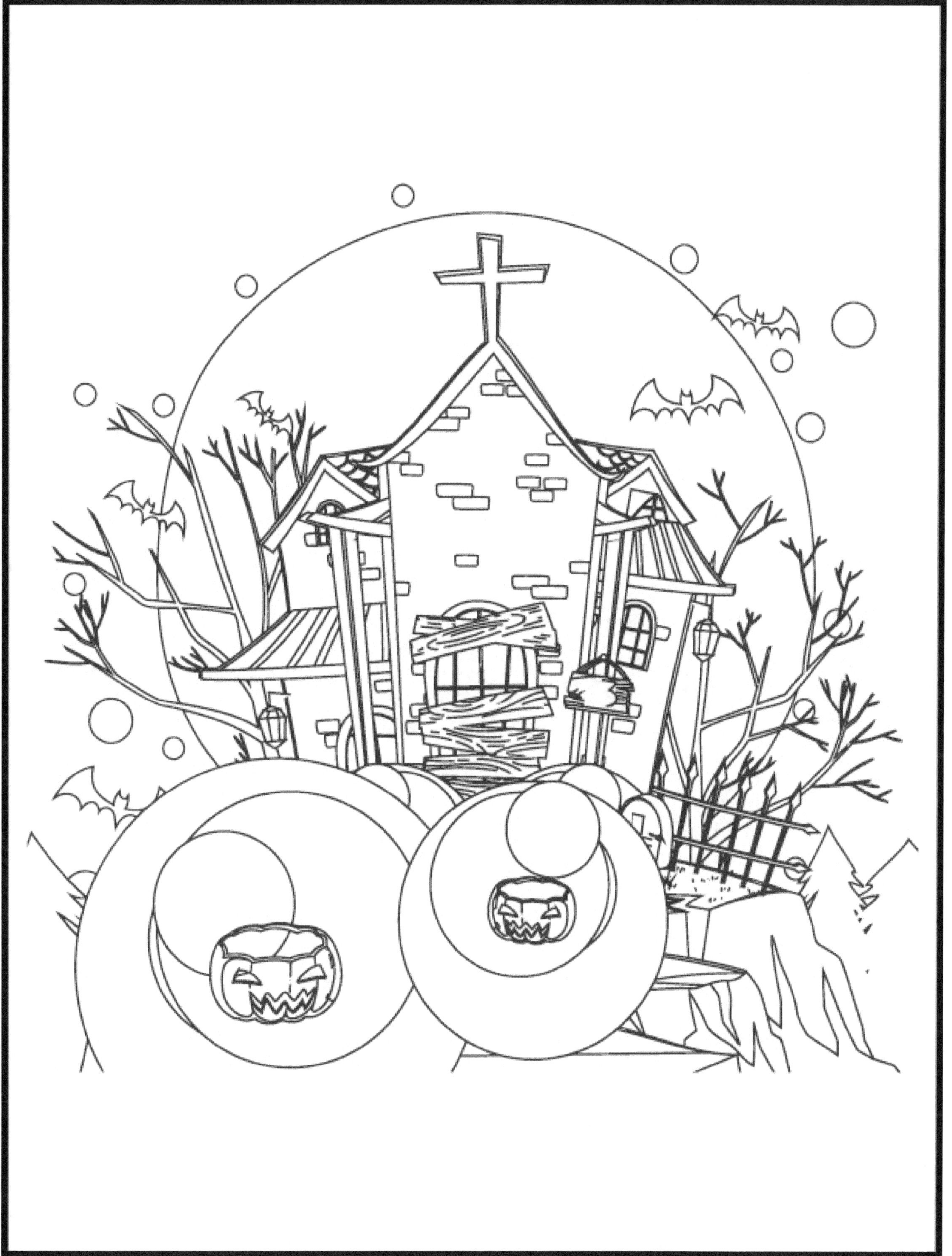

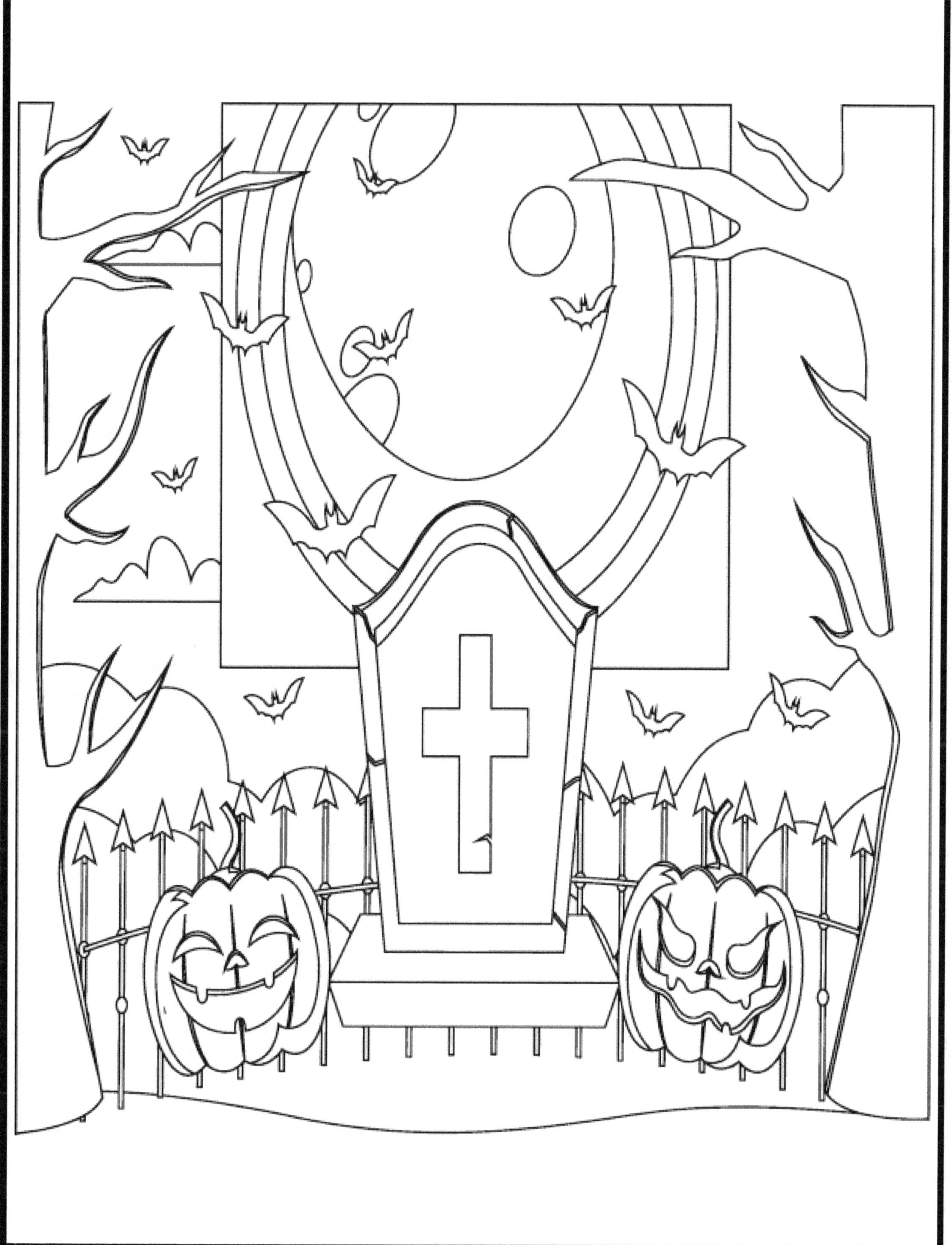

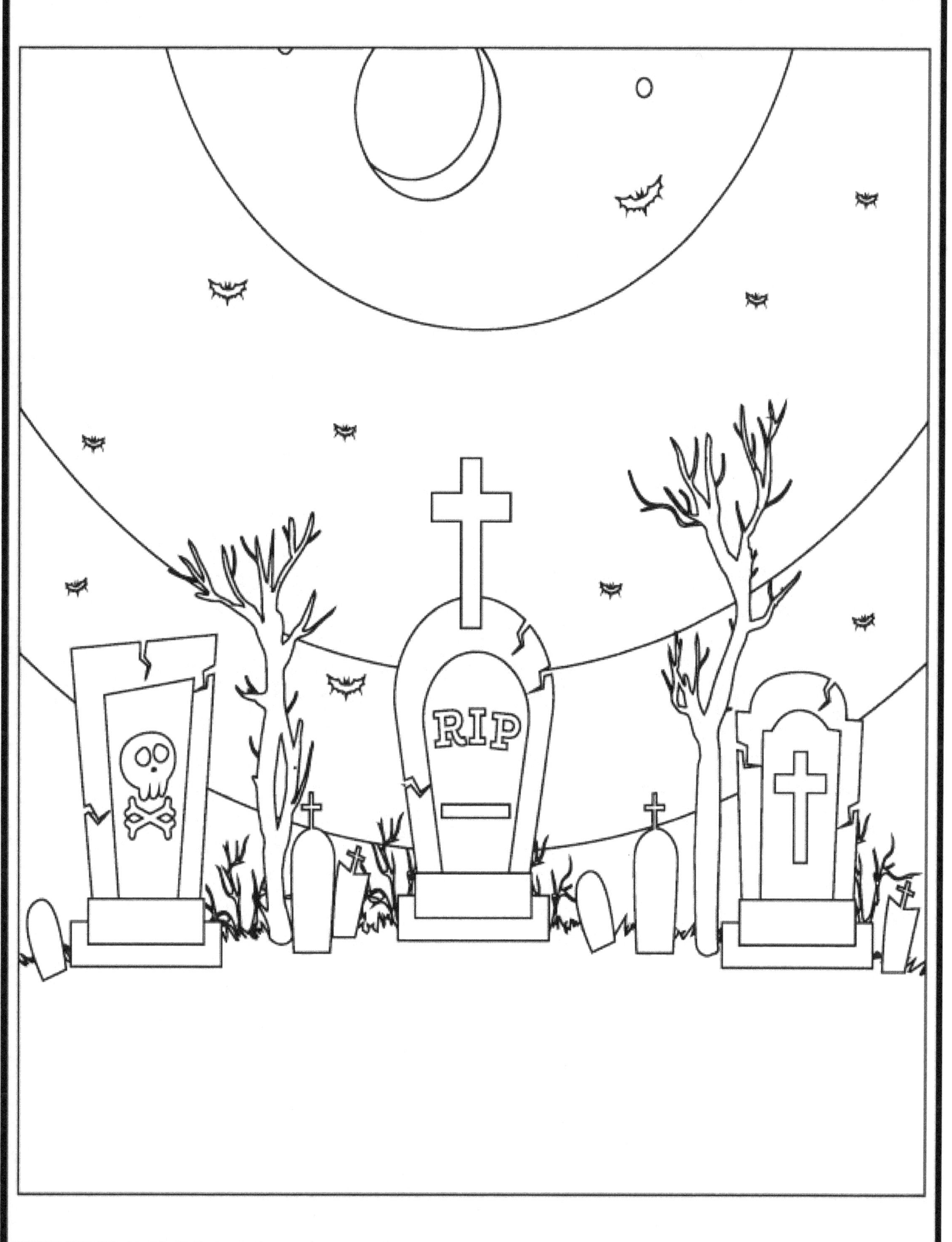

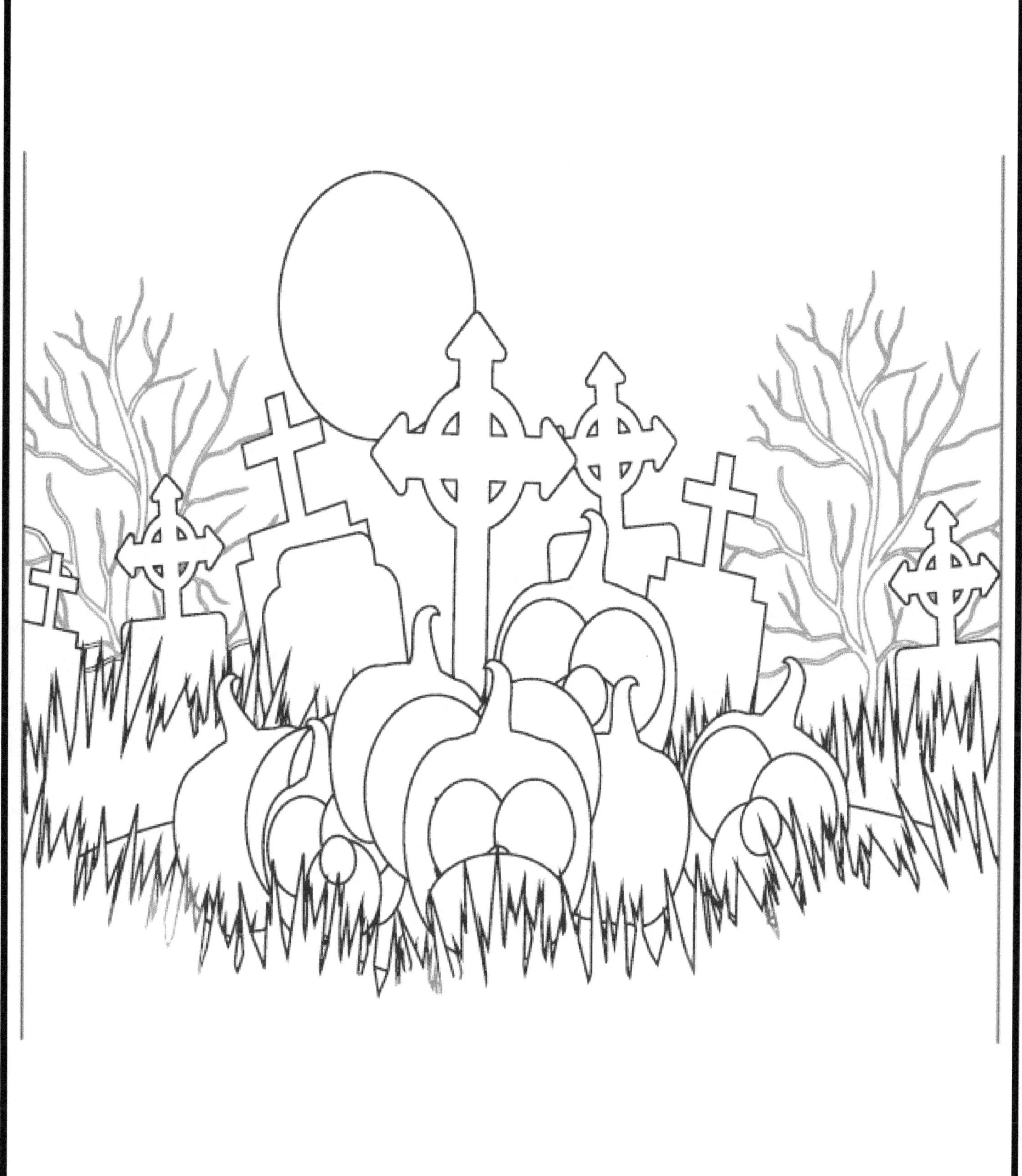

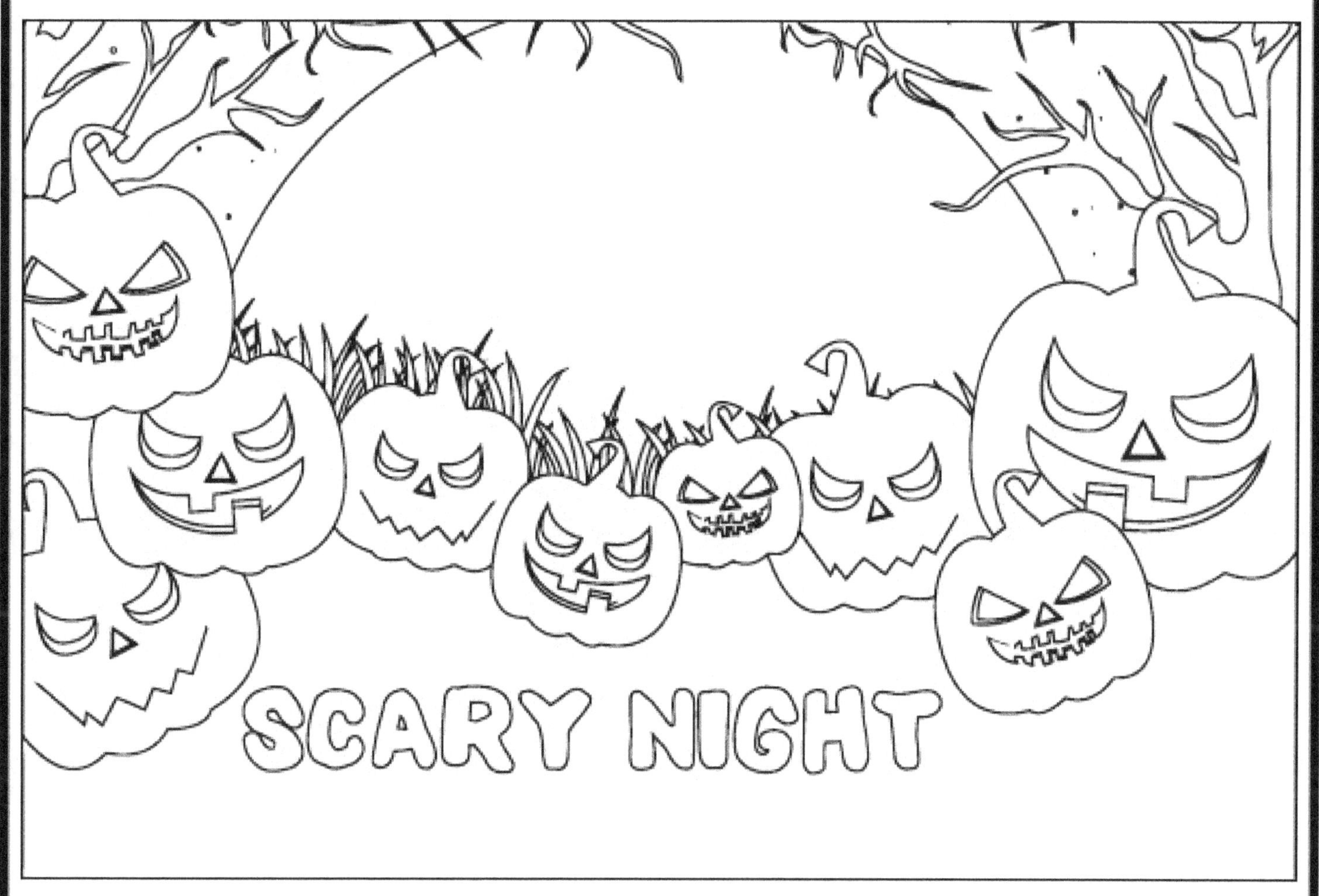
SCARY NIGHT

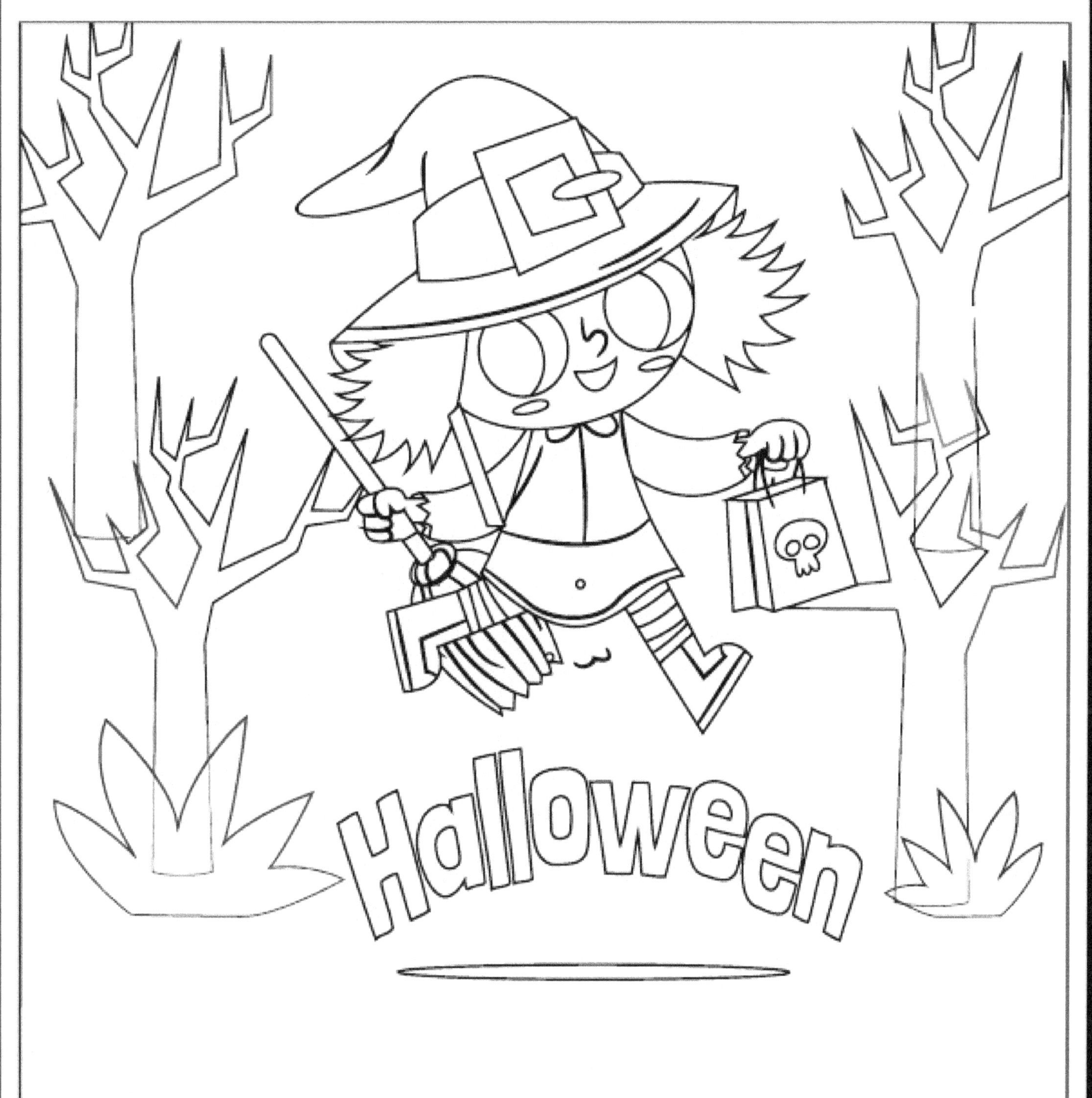

Halloween

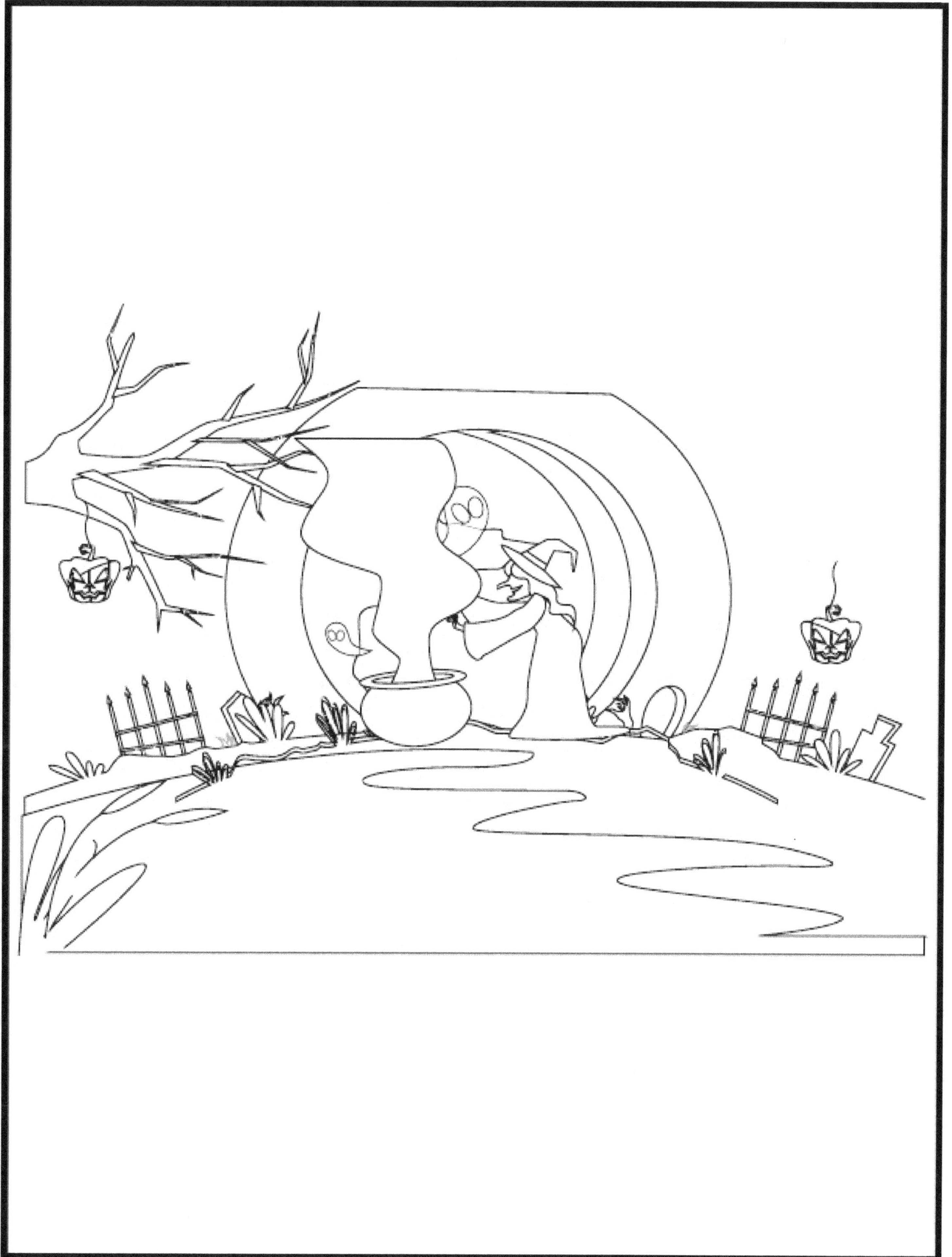

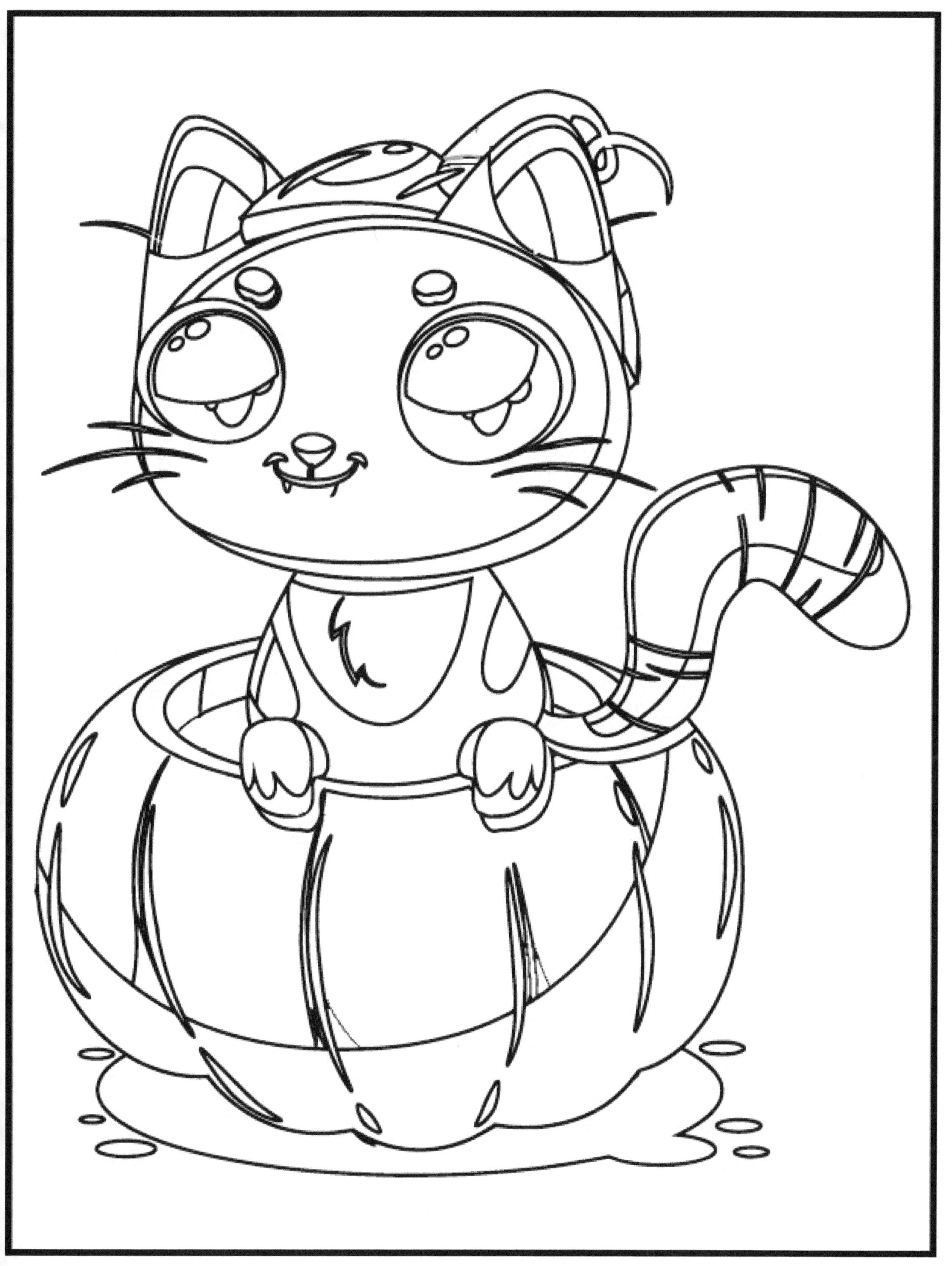

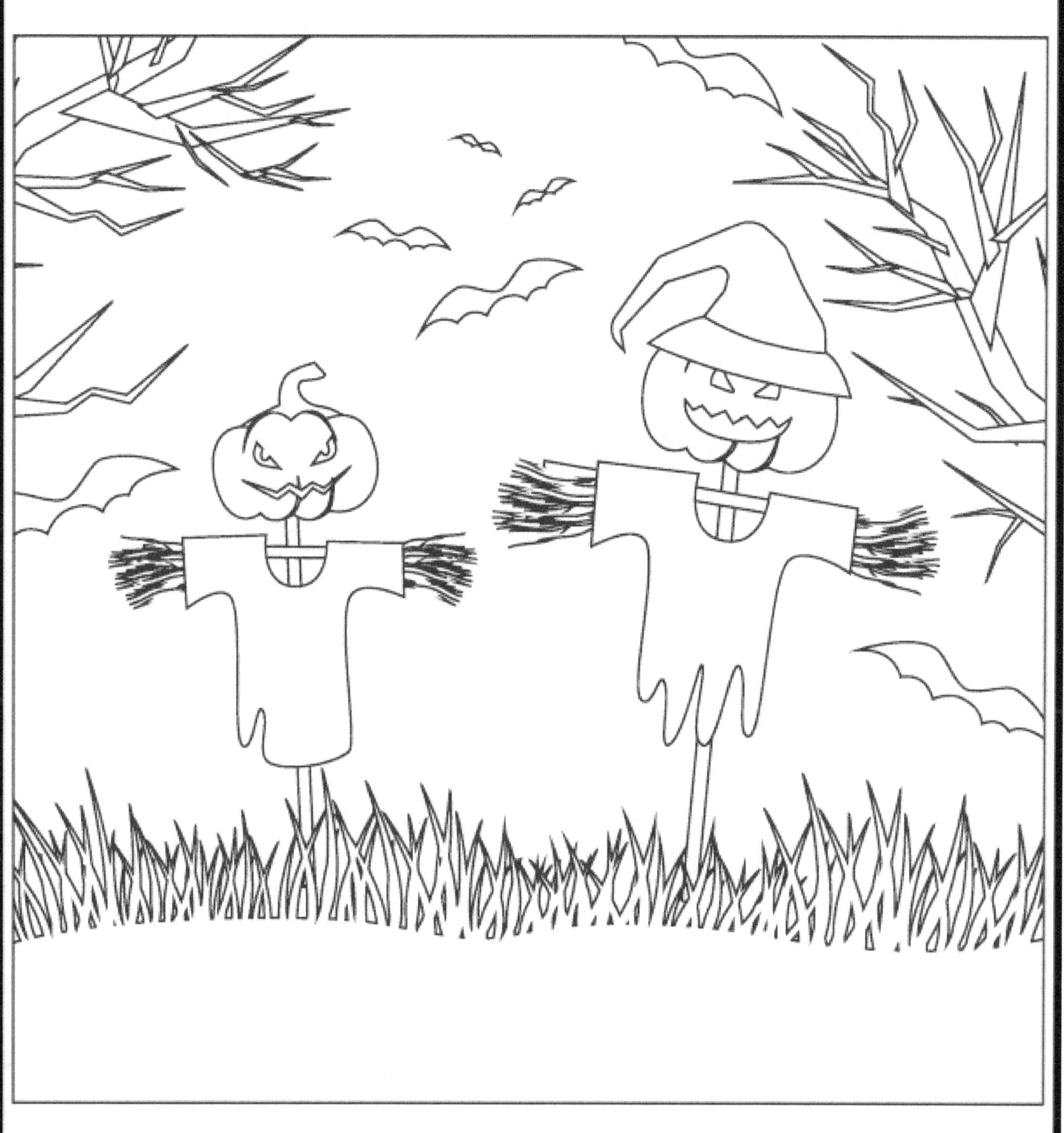

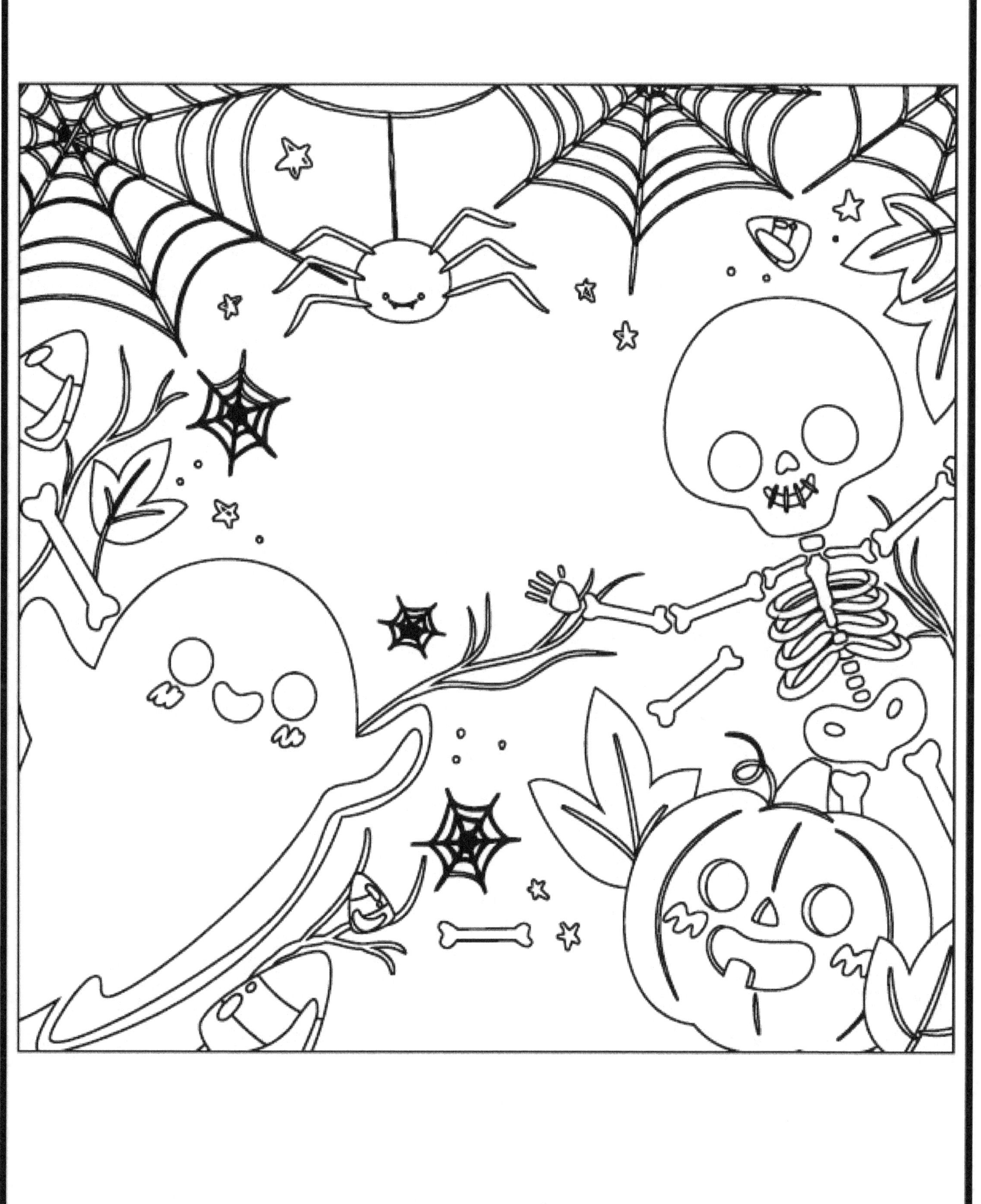

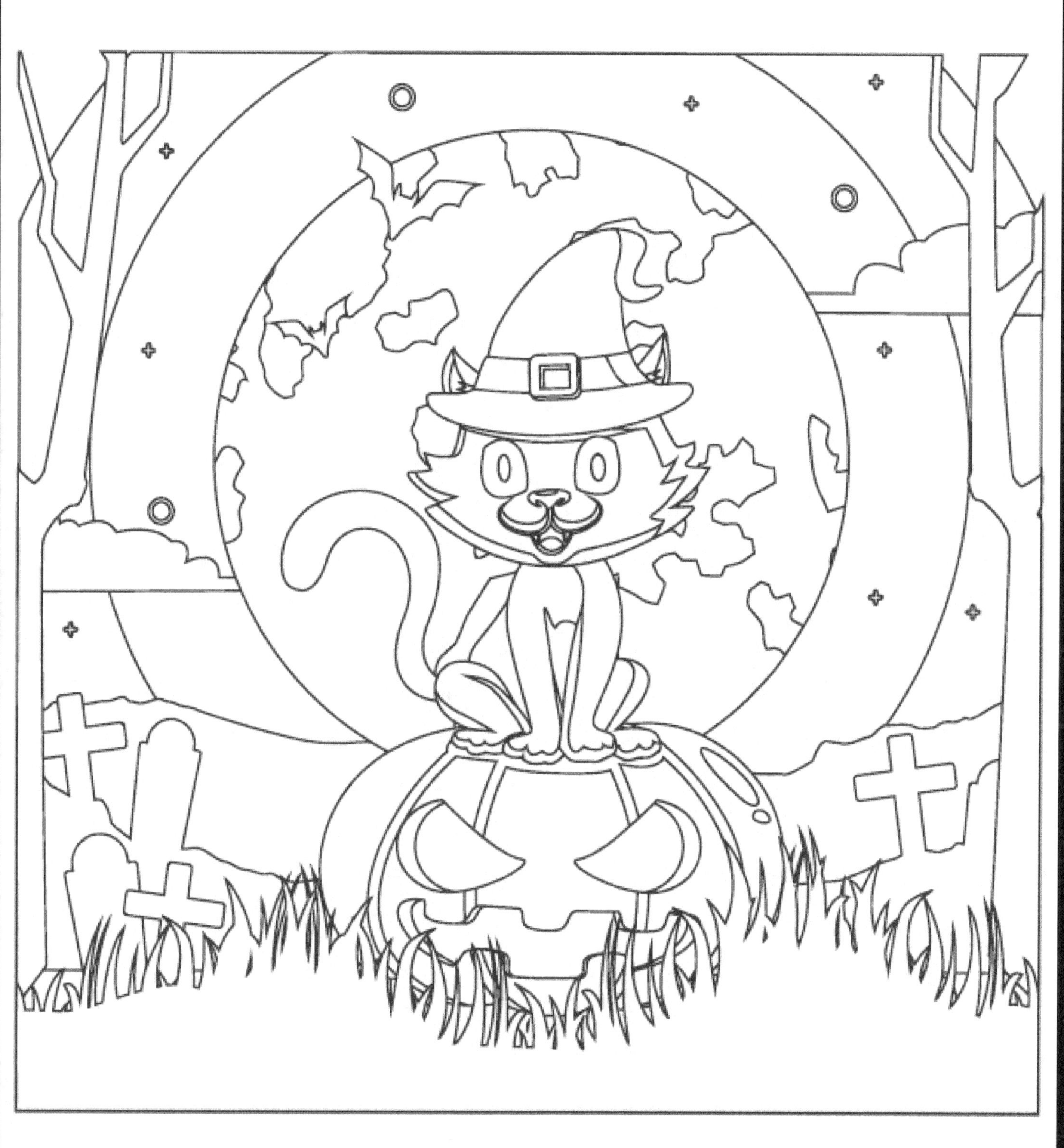

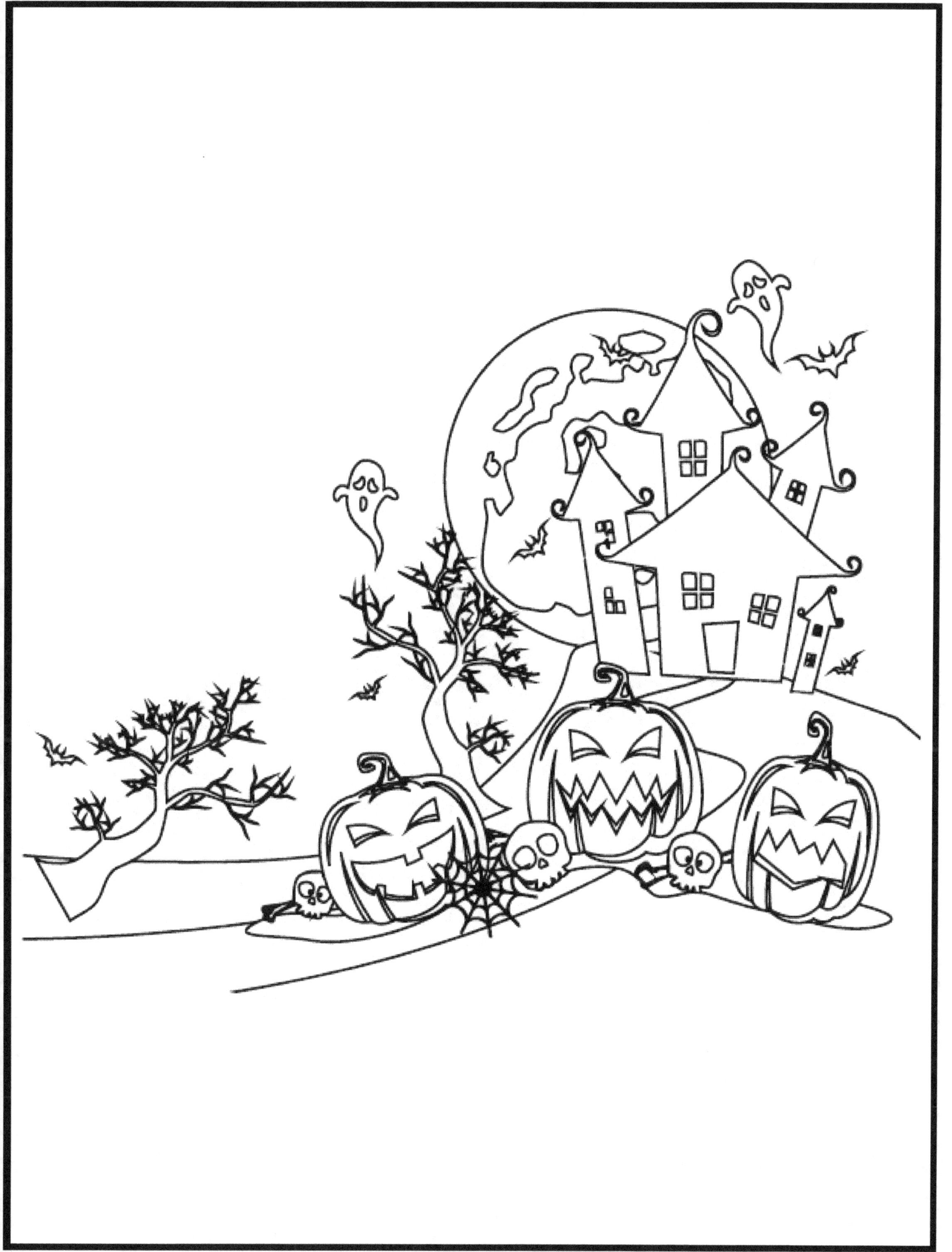

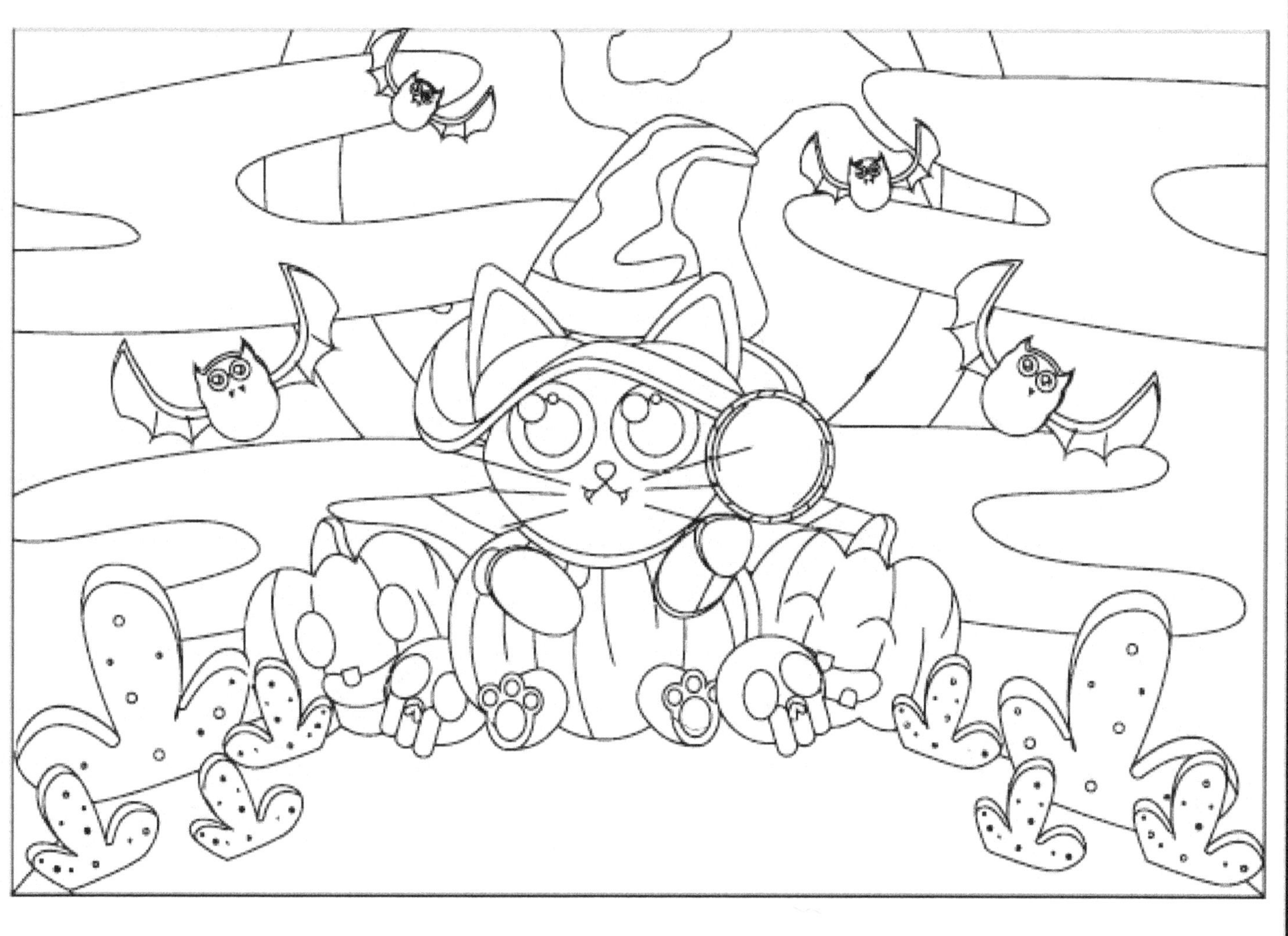

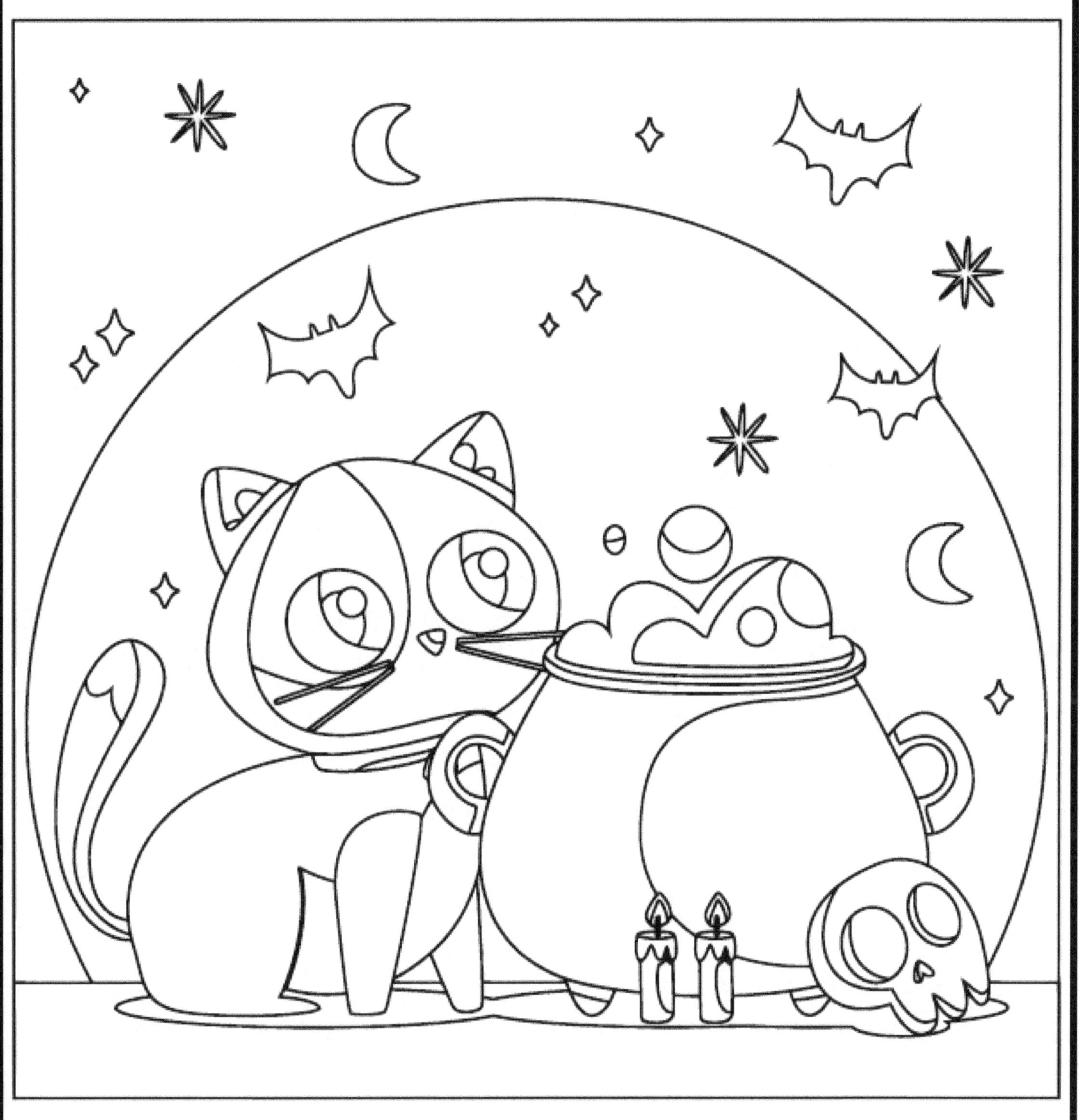

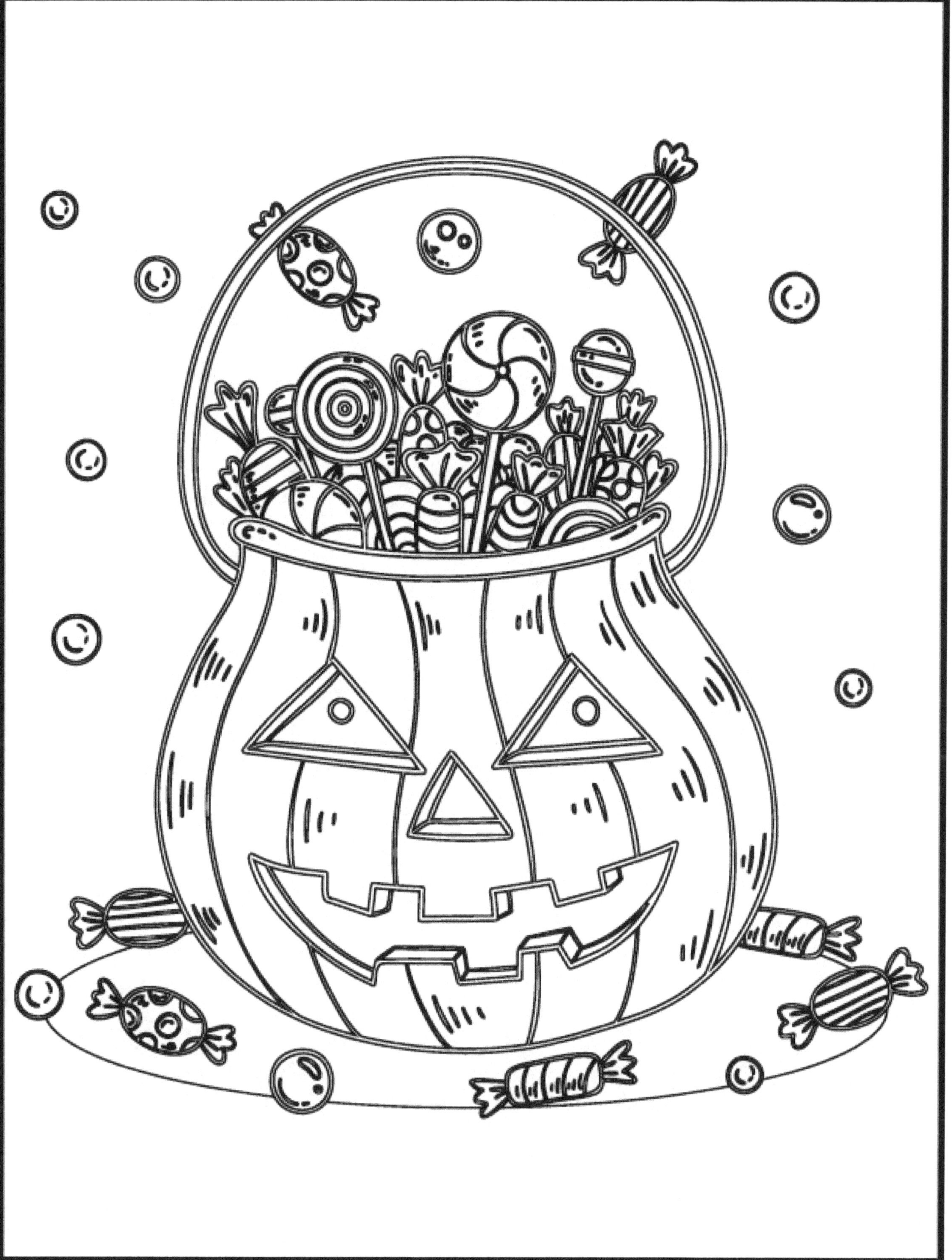

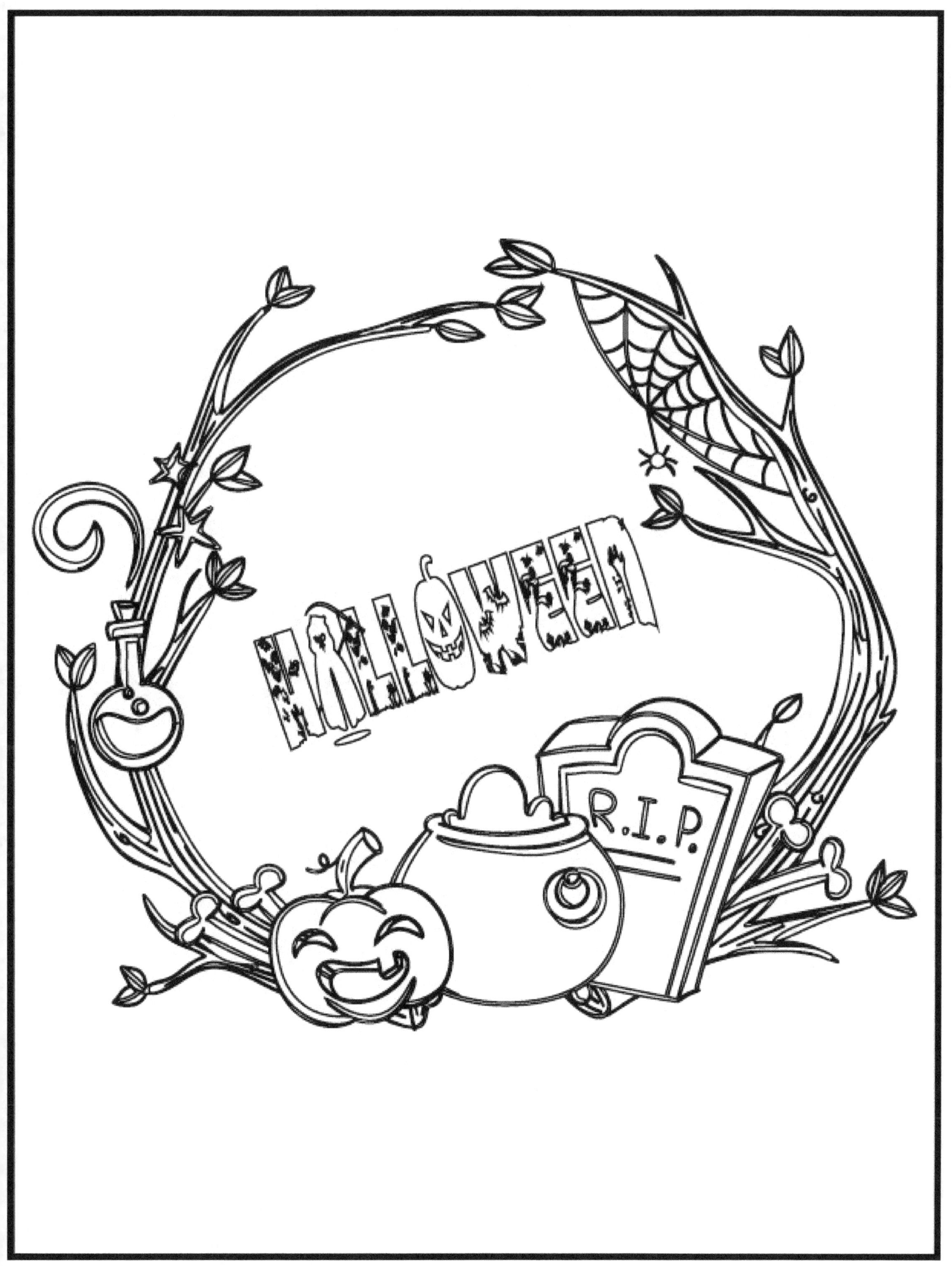

HALLOWEEN
R.I.P.